From the Trenches to Classrooms

From the Trenches to Classrooms

Continuing Education
at Case Western Reserve University
and the Evolution of ACE

Paula Coppedge

Eagle Creek Press
Solon, Ohio

Eagle Creek Press
32513 Seneca Drive
Solon, OH 44139

ISBN: 0-9759366-1-1

Printed by BookMasters, Inc., Mansfield, Ohio

DEDICATION

Carolyn Sutphin Leitch was a human dynamo who headed the Case Western Reserve University Book Sale for more than 25 years. Her dedication and physical labor on its behalf were phenomenal. Her willingness to do any leftover tasks and to work longer, harder, and faster than anyone else was not a myth.

Carolyn (Mrs. Robert Leitch) was a native Clevelander, a graduate of Laurel School and the Flora Stone Mather College for Women of Western Reserve University. After graduating from Mather, she decided to take some practical courses and enrolled at downtown Cleveland College. With her interest in education, it was only natural for her to find the Women's Association of Cleveland College (WACC).

Carolyn loved books and understood the need for adult education. As an active member of WACC, she served on the Education Committee and was a member-at-large on the WACC board. Then she was swept up by the Book Sale, the fund-raiser for WACC.

In 1968, her garage was used as a West Side collection drop-off for books. It became apparent to her that many more books could be sold if an easier way could be found for collecting, sorting, and storing them. When she began chairing the Book Sale's Collection Committee, she solicited help from the Society National Bank. The bank allowed the Women's Association to put large, painted cardboard boxes for book donations in some of its branches. Volunteers

Carolyn Sutphin Leitch
1926 -1993

would check and empty the donation boxes weekly. Carolyn and other workers bought heavy-duty station wagons so they could haul the books. This wonderful cooperative effort lasted about 15 years. The boxes not only brought in the books but also advertised the Book Sale itself. Bank managers grew to expect the big, yellow boxes in the spring.

In 1972, when Carolyn became "head honcho," "The Sale" was tremendously successful, grossing more than $8,000. However, this intense woman with a nervous little laugh had board members squirming when she chastised them for giving little support. Instead, the Book Sale relied on nonmembers and their families to do the work. So impressed were the board members that many rallied and went on to become longtime Book Sale volunteers. The dedication of Carolyn's family and friends continues, as many still come to help with the sale.

Carolyn's philosophy was to find a job that interested a particular volunteer and then leave her or him alone, probably immersed knee-deep in books. If someone was reluctant to accept the position, she would find someone else. She would stay out of the way, offering help only when needed. Instead, she used her time and efforts picking up the loose ends—from parking passes to hot meals. Workers responded by volunteering repeatedly, thereby becoming more knowledgeable and valuable to the sale. Carolyn could and did any and all jobs. Her kicks came from finding marvelous gems of books and getting them to new homes. So many books were available to so many people that working the actual days of the sale was exhilarating! Seeing the smiling faces of the customers leaving with their arms loaded with books was a thrill.

Carolyn had a hand in everything and was always game to try new ideas. One of her inspirations was a silent auction. She thought that on the slow and boring third day of the sale she would have an auction of some of the unusual and interesting items that might possibly be valuable. Everyone would have a chance to bid. Frequently the items were ones that were difficult to price: Shirley Temple paper dolls, Paul Newman's schoolbooks, an early copy of *The Simple Cobbler of Aggawam*, a Beethoven score of *Fidelio* from 1828. The Carolyn Sutphin Leitch Silent Auction has now become a high point in the sale.

Carolyn had a clear view of the world. Things were in black and white with very few shades of gray. The need for good relationships with the university was so important to her that she, by herself, repacked hundreds of leftover books that had been tossed all over the gym. She was not timid about asking for help from alumni, the university, Society National Bank, WACC (ACE) members, Senior Scholars, or the general public. She seemed a bit embarrassed when thanked for a job well done.

Knowing how important reading was for many people, Carolyn managed to redistribute thousands of books. Her example of dedication and hard work was awesome. This project was a tiny facet of her life that addressed the challenges of education and literacy. No one has any idea of how much or how many lives she touched and influenced. Her service to the community at large, especially the literate community, is unparalleled. With her death, the world lost a marvelous, compassionate human being.

–Nancy Fleming

Nancy Fleming cochaired
the Book Sale for 20 years.

This publication was underwritten by the Carolyn Sutphin Leitch Memorial Fund.

ACKNOWLEDGMENTS

Many thanks to the CWRU archives, whose helpful librarians were invaluable hunters for information; Marjorie Johnson, who provided time-consuming assistance, helpful criticism, and encouragement and who masterminded publication; Pam Hume, whose careful reading prevented historical inaccuracies; Nancy Fleming, a discerning editor who helped solve organizational problems; Mary Jo Groppe, whose keen eye for an awkward construction smoothed out the rough spots; and certainly the ACE office staff.

CONTENTS

From the Trenches to Classrooms

WHAT TO DO WITH THE DOUGHBOYS?

Western Reserve University's venture into adult education began not in Cleveland but in France after the 1918 armistice, as Newton Diehl Baker, Wilson's Secretary of War and Cleveland's former mayor, wrestled with the problem of keeping 2 million restless doughboys out of trouble. The fighting was over and the soldiers were stranded in Europe with nothing to do while they waited for ships to take them home. Britain, France, and the U.S. Department of War feared the worst. General Pershing's army proposed to drill them until they dropped, hoping at the same time to work out solutions to the past errors of the Meuse-Argonne offensive. Secretary Baker considered that a pointless exercise for soldiers about to be demobilized. Nevertheless some way to keep the men peaceably occupied had to be found.

While the Allies abandoned themselves to a frenzied celebration of the armistice, Secretary Baker brooded over the problem, wondering whether perhaps a few of the men might like to enroll in college-level courses if instructors could be found. He asked for a show of interest and, to his astonishment, got an overwhelming response. Many of the doughboys realized that lack of education not only had prevented their promotions but also would hinder their advancement in civilian life.

Baker had his solution, one born out of utter desperation. It allayed the fears of the Europeans and resulted in the establishment of a postwar educational program for the stranded armed forces. In addition, it unleashed a revolutionary concept of adult education that had an enormous influence on both the city of Cleveland and Western Reserve University. Ultimately it brought about the university's groundbreaking, lasting partnership with the voluntary organization that is now the Association for Continuing Education.

In France and England, schools for the military were hastily established in unused hospitals, in vacant sheds, in any space available that was out of the weather. The relieved French and British were easily persuaded to open the doors of their universities to qualified American servicemen. Thus, the University of the American Expeditionary Forces in France was born,

Newton D. Baker served as mayor of Cleveland from 1912 to 1916 and as the U.S. Secretary of War during World War I, but he is best remembered among Association for Continuing Education devotees for founding Cleveland College as an institution promoting adult learning.

augmented by Post Schools that provided education at the elementary and high school levels. The UAEF bore little resemblance to any traditional college. The khaki College of Beaune was housed in temporary shacks with only blackboards, platforms, and chairs for equipment. Soldiers with academic backgrounds volunteered to teach classes. In one school, Baker found a mere private lecturing on integral calculus to 20 officers. Military rank bowed to academic proficiency.

There had been nothing like it in the history of the world—soldiers laying down their bayonets and taking up books. The poet Edgar Lee Masters, in a burst of idealistic enthusiasm, applauded Baker's program, writing that an army with ideas would make an army with guns superfluous. Before the University of the American Expeditionary Forces ended, 11,000 students had been enrolled in 11 colleges, with 130,000 more in the Post Schools, to say nothing of those who subscribed to the correspondence schools that taught liberal arts, law, medicine and dentistry.

The enthusiastic reception of his efforts to prevent American soldiers from creating havoc among America's allies changed Baker's life. It reinforced his life-long conviction that people were eager to better themselves and that, if the means of doing so were put within their grasp, they might continue to learn throughout their lives.

Back in the United States and retired from the cabinet, Baker returned to his Cleveland law practice but continued his advocacy of adult education. He had been active in politics before the war, first as law director and later as mayor of Cleveland under the tutelage of the municipal reformer, Mayor Tom L. Johnson. Baker had been much impressed by the tent meetings Tom Johnson had held in order to get himself elected mayor four times, conducting public forums in an enormous tent that seated 5,000 people. He moved it from ward to ward in the city before elections, taking issues directly to the voters, keeping the public fully informed of problems and plans, and encouraging debate. The Cleveland electorate was said to be the best-informed in the nation in the early 1900s and Cleveland "the best governed city in America," according to author Lincoln Steffens.

With this example before him, reinforced by his experience in postwar Europe, Baker resolved to make it possible for the ex-soldiers to continue their schooling as private citizens and to do so even while fulfilling adult responsibilities. In 1924 he persuaded the Cleveland Foundation to sponsor a survey of higher education in the city, the results of which produced a recommendation for the establishment of a *downtown college* to provide day and evening classes that would be accessible to working adults as either full- or part-time students. It was to be called Cleveland College and managed under the direction of Western Reserve University with the cooperation of Case Institute of Applied Science, long before the eventual merger of the two institutions. The new college would establish a comprehensive adult education program offering credit courses in the late afternoon and evening for part-time students, as well as develop a degree program in business administration to complement the liberal arts and engineering curricula offered at University Circle. This latter program was, in embryonic form, the Weatherhead School of Management, which is now housed in Frank Gehry's shining Peter B. Lewis Building.

In the Beginning

The Board of Trustees consisted of the president and secretary-treasurer of WRU, four Case trustees, four WRU trustees, and two others—12 in all, with Baker as chairman of the board. The infant school had almost no endowment, but Baker persuaded Ellen Scripps of the California newspaper and real estate fortune to contribute $25,000 to pay for the charter. He found 90 Clevelanders willing to underwrite the project to the extent of $500 each. This gave Cleveland College enough financial security so that under Ohio law it could be established as a degree-granting institution. Western Reserve loaned Wilfred R. Leutner, dean of administration, to Cleveland College to become its acting director.

The board moved fast. Cleveland College was chartered in July 1925 and opened its doors in September, only two months later. Although WRU and Case declined to assume financial responsibility, they permitted free use of laboratories during evening hours and allowed faculty members to be employed part-time to teach Cleveland College evening classes. The boards of trustees were interlocking, but WRU appointed the director and underwrote degrees.

Not only had Baker spearheaded the movement to establish this downtown adult college, he did much to ensure its survival. When the presidency of WRU fell vacant, his position as a trustee enabled him to influence the selection of a replacement, one, he hoped, whose willingness to venture into untried paths would be vital for the development of the fledgling school. Baker's choice was Robert E. Vinson, who had attracted his notice during World War I, when Vinson, as president of the University of Texas, had used government funding to make the school into a major training camp for military aeronautics, as well as aviation and automobile mechanics. Vinson was a fearless, somewhat less than circumspect crusader, whose University of Texas presidency had been marked by bitter feuds with Texas Governor James E. Ferguson, a conservative banker and demagogue. In 1917 Ferguson had vetoed the entire appropriation for the university and then grudgingly offered Vinson $2 million on condition that he fire six professors whom Ferguson found objectionable. The outraged Vinson, joined by anti-Ferguson forces that included lawyers, newspaper editors, and university alumni, put detectives on Ferguson's trail, finding massive misuse of funds and ultimately bringing about Ferguson's impeachment and removal from office. Unshackled, Vinson then secured raises for the faculty and quadrupled the value and quality of the library. But his administration was in effect a war against the state government, which held the purse strings, and in 1921 the Texas legislature broke up his programs, setting the University of Texas back many years.

Thus, in 1923 Vinson was happy to accept the presidency of Western Reserve, his candidacy enthusiastically backed by Newton D. Baker, who remembered the vigorous young university president who had cooperated so ably with the War Department. Vinson delighted in innovation and vigorously advanced the policies of the struggling new downtown college.

In 1925-1926, its first year of operation, 108 classes were conducted with a total enrollment of 1,496. The faculty, mostly from WRU and Case, as well as part-time lecturers from the business community, consisted of one full-time and 63 part-time instructors. Classes met in three rented floors over an automobile agency at 20th and Euclid. With great satisfaction Baker saw the enrollment quadruple in four years. The college ran out of space and had to borrow classrooms wherever it could find them—Lakewood and Cleveland Heights high schools, the Cleveland Public Library, the YWCA, the Red Cross Teaching Center, the Museum of Natural History. Students ranged in age from 18 to 80, and the college attracted national recognition as a leader in adult education.

The trustees' mission went far beyond the provision of undergraduate instruction leading to a bachelor's degree. The board aimed to establish a school

6

that rose above the immaturity of conventional classrooms in contrast to one that addressed itself to the needs of recent high school graduates. The board's creation was to be an educational center where students of all ages and backgrounds could study, provided only that they had a real desire to learn. In the founders' philosophy, education was a process that continued throughout life, rather than a course of study terminated by a degree. The education they envisioned would be fueled by the enthusiasm of adult minds in quest of intellectual growth, a process that

Robert E. Vinson served as president of Western Reserve University from 1923 to 1933.

would continue throughout life for everyone. Men and women would be encouraged to study, if not for a degree, then surely for the satisfaction of cultural, vocational, civic, or recreational needs.

Baker saw Cleveland College as an outgrowth of Tom L. Johnson's tent meetings, an institution intended to make every adult Clevelander understand the economic, social, and political outlines of modern government. Remembering the rioting of jobless veterans after World War I, he also hoped that in hard times the college would provide insurance against the "rebellious sentiments aroused by hardship," especially because of the college's close relation with "unfortunate people of radical propensities."

NEWTON D. BAKER'S BABY

'Don't become a mental mummy.
Take courses at Cleveland College
and make yourself interesting to others.'

Baker's avocation was education. At one time he was a trustee of seven universities and colleges, including Western Reserve, which he served from 1916 until his death in 1937, part of the time as chairman of the board. He was offered the presidencies of the University of Michigan, Johns Hopkins, and the University of Virginia, but he declined them all. Cleveland College was for him the most significant educational project with which he had been connected. His zeal in pursuing it was evangelical. He wrote:

"If we are to study the economic problems of the future dispassionately; if we are not to have purely materialistic ideals; if the fruits of our material achievements are to be cultural blessings to us; if we are envisioning a world in which it is safe for America to be and in which she can be at her best; then it seems to me that we must continue the process of education indefinitely. We must aim at *every adult person* in this country an education that he cannot escape, and that, when it has found its mark and hit him, will drive him from his reliance on passions and prejudices and make him a citizen of the Greek kind."

He saw liberal education as vital to democracy, particularly in the United States, whose cosmopolitan population needed a common body of shared knowledge and understanding to bind it together. Because collegiate education was becoming increasingly overspecialized, it was the responsibility of adult education to provide the common core of liberal education that men and women were not getting from colleges that had become degree factories.

The 1926 catalog stated that Cleveland College's intention was to become part of the "Greater University of Cleveland," but plans bogged down in disputes between Case and Reserve. Nevertheless, Cleveland College was able to maintain its own board of trustees until 1942 and was zealous in retaining its own identity and options for future growth.

It was immediately apparent that a school of this size and nature would need more than spare-time attention from WRU administrators. President Vinson offered the directorship of the year-old college to a former Texas colleague, Alexander Caswell Ellis, who had been a professor of the philosophy of education at the University of Texas from 1897 to 1926 and was one of the profes-

This March 1932 Cleveland News rendering captures the unique personality of Alexander Caswell Ellis, the first director of Cleveland College. In addition to leading the institution for adult learning from 1926 to 1941, the newspaper noted that Ellis taught "police the tricks of jiu-jitsu" and that "his pet hobby is agriculture."

sors whose dismissal had been an issue in the war between Vinson and Governor Ferguson. Ellis was a man of inexhaustible and wide-ranging energy, which he devoted to causes as diverse as adult education, rural health care, prison reform, conservation of natural resources, and women's suffrage, but whose enthusiasm occasionally led him to intemperate speech. His Texas job had been jeopardized after he referred to Governor Ferguson as "the iridescent jackass" with a "booze ring of cutthroats behind him" who had packed the board of regents with a bunch of "gamblers, libertines and brewery lawyers ..." and, on top of that, added Ellis indignantly, *he dismissed me and five other leading members of the faculty.*" He was saved by President Vinson's offer of the directorship of Cleveland College.

Ellis had only contempt for traditional institutions filled with "immature college boys and girls" and campuses dominated by "unscholarly, if not infantile interests in athletics, fraternities, college politics, and other such extra-intellectual activities." By 1928 Ellis could crow that his "homeless 3-year-old night school with absolutely nothing to attract students except the teaching of its faculty" was registering more students than "all four of the well-equipped local day colleges" —Baldwin-Wallace, John Carroll, and Western Reserve University's Adelbert and Flora Stone Mather colleges.

These well-established institutions, which could not bring themselves to regard Cleveland College as a legitimate school much less as an equal and a competitor, were horrified by Ellis' language and shameless proselytism. He wrote flamboyant advertisements proclaiming the advantages of adult education as a lifelong experience, in contrast to the usual campus with its four-year programs for post-adolescents. "The art of mummifying the body has been rediscovered," he wrote. "The art of mummifying the mind was never lost. Don't become a mental mummy. Take courses at Cleveland College and make yourself interesting to others." He went so far as to send recruiting letters to Lake Erie College students and their parents, stressing the decadence of traditional education—to the considerable indignation of both the Lake Erie administration and the parents.

The students and faculty of Cleveland College represented a new breed. Most students were gainfully employed in the city, many of them in jobs arranged by the college in its work-study program. Because many faculty members had been recruited from the business world, they divided their time between teaching

10

This 1947 photo shows the first real home of Cleveland College at the Chamber of Commerce building on Public Square.

and business or professional activity and brought real, practical knowledge into the classroom. Said the catalog: "Cleveland College is intended to minister to the higher vocational, professional, and cultural needs of those for whom the typical college is inaccessible or not well adapted." Thus it addressed, among others, married women with duties at home, men who had families to support, working men and women, youngsters who couldn't afford a residential institution, and high-level business executives seeking specialized knowledge.

Clevelanders had so abundantly justified Baker's vision that still more space had to be found. In 1929 the college moved to ample new quarters in the seven-story Chamber of Commerce building on Public Square next to the Society for Savings Bank, a site now occupied by the Key Tower. Enrollment reached 7,116, a 60 percent increase over the previous year, and the future looked rosy.

At that time , Adelbert and especially Mather colleges of Western Reserve University maintained rigid admission policies that denied acceptance to both part-time and transfer students. But Cleveland College offered a way around this ban because any of its students who were academically qualified and wished to transfer into either of Western Reserve's undergraduate colleges could do so. In addition, the young people who were unable for financial or social reasons to attend other colleges found that Cleveland College's work/study program, which was a fertile recruiting ground for employers, enabled them to take college courses, work toward degrees and, at the same time, hold jobs that paid their way.

The college's Division of Extension Education reached out into the community by offering six- to eight-week courses serving the needs of such organizations as the Cleveland Board of Education, the Social Hygiene Association, the Red Cross Teaching Center, and the Association for Public Health and Parent Education. It offered a program in radio education administered by Grazella Pulliver Shepherd, later the director of general studies, and two-day institutes on marriage, probation, child welfare, and international relations. Newton D. Baker himself taught an international affairs course.

CRISIS

'... the nation or community that neglects
adult education does so at its peril.'

But disaster was in store. Only months later, the stock market crashed, banks closed, businesses failed, and enrollment dropped to 3,000 by the next year. Deficits grew. By 1932 the deficit was more than $100,000, the college was in arrears for another $100,000 in rent to the Chamber of Commerce, and the school was to lose $32,000 when the Guardian Trust failed to reopen after the bank holiday in March 1933. Borrowing was out of the question, for nowhere was there money to be lent. There were no funds to pay the faculty, who had already suffered salary cuts of 25 percent to 40 percent and had been advised to seek employment elsewhere. President Vinson told Ellis to close Cleveland College downtown and move as many night classes as possible to University Circle.

This meant the death of the young college, and Newton D. Baker couldn't bear it. He rushed to its rescue and told the trustees that he would give up all outside activity to devote every spare minute to raising money for Cleveland College. As he put it, he was scratching not only his head but the bottom of his pocket in an attempt to keep the college alive. He persuaded the Carnegie Foundation to give $50,000. He got $20,000 more from four "men of purse." He sent out a general appeal to alumni and friends, which netted $30,000, and Baker himself, although not a wealthy man, lent and donated several thousand dollars. All in all, it was a remarkable achievement in the midst of the Great Depression, when jobless working men were joining bread lines and ruined investors were throwing themselves out of skyscraper windows. Enrollment, of course, dropped. In 1933 it was less than 3,000. Case terminated its affiliation in 1934, and the Division of Extension Education ceased to exist except for radio education and some international affairs classes.

Enrollment recovered in the late 1930s, but during World War II it fell again to just over 3,000. Ellis said 15 years at Cleveland College was like "walking a tightrope over a financial Niagara Falls every year" because in the absence of substantial en-

When financial disasters threatened Cleveland College's existence in 1932, Newton D. Baker came to the rescue of his beloved institution. As this 1937 Plain Dealer photo notes, this was Baker's most characteristic pose while he was in public office.

dowment it was forced to rely on tuition for more than 80 percent of its operating expenses. The young institution's fortunes had indeed fluctuated dramatically. It flourished for its first five years but struggled with serious problems for the next 15. From 1930 to 1945, it had a net deficit of $150,000 and was $530,000 in arrears in rent.

But Ellis' faith in its mission was unabated. His final report in 1941 developed his favorite theme that youth cannot possibly learn everything it needs to know by the age of 21. "Youth is neither equipped nor motivated for such learning. If what I have said is correct, then adult education is not just a pleasant diversion, nor is it an education merely to help those who did not have adequate educational opportunities in youth, but it is a serious and essential part of the education of every adult, of you and of me, no matter how many colleges we attended or how many degrees we took in our youth; and the nation or community that neglects adult education does so at its peril. It may be that nothing but adult education can save our civilization from a complete collapse; it may be that we are now actually in the midst of a race between adult education and disaster."

During World War II, Cleveland College housed the War Training Office of WRU, giving engineering, science, and management courses to more than 6,000 factory and office personnel engaged in war work. It was one of the few institutions chosen by the Military Government Division of the War Department to conduct a Civil Affairs Training School.

Postwar Renaissance

*'the men and women who are carrying
the economic, social and political
responsibilities of adults in our culture'*

At the end of the war in 1945, the G.I. Bill of Rights, one of the best pieces of legislation ever passed by the Congress, rewarded veterans' years of service with an equivalent period of free tuition and college expenses. The bill had been designed as an expedient to prevent a repetition of the riots by unemployed ex-soldiers that had unsettled the country after the first World War, but it did far more than preserve the peace. It proved, beyond the wildest dreams of its sponsors, to be of enormous benefit to the whole country. The flood of college-educated veterans it released into the national economy dramatically added to the intellectual capital of the United States. And it brought ex-servicemen flocking to Cleveland College.

To respond to their needs, an expanded board of trustees formed hard-working subcommittees whose rosters read like a *Who's Who* of Cleveland business and professional people. So did the list of "lecturers," as the part-time lay faculty members recruited from outside the ranks of academia were called. They were knowledgeable people with successful careers, leaders in their fields, whose daily experience of the world gave them excellent qualifications to prepare their students for useful positions.

This 1945 photo captures Cleveland College, the school for adults, during its heyday.

Banking was taught by the head of the statistical department of the Society for Savings Bank and by a department head at the Federal Reserve Bank. Accounting was taught by the founding partners of Walthall and Drake accounting firm and by the head of the trust department at the Cleveland Trust. Radio was taught by the program directors at WGAR and WBOE, real estate by the attorney for the city planning commission, a professional real estate appraiser, and the vice president of Joseph Laronge real estate firm.

The journalism department boasted Plain Dealer staff members, the city editor of the Cleveland Press, and Howard Preston, a highly regarded Cleveland News columnist. The director of B'nai B'rith Hillel Foundation taught history.

17

From the Trenches to Classrooms

Robert Rawson, who held a doctorate in political science and was the vice president of Empire Plow, taught political science. Prominent architect Joseph Ceruti, who left his mark notably on Shaker Square, taught architecture, as did the chief draftsmen of several architectural firms.

The business marketing department had as lecturers the local manager of American Airlines, the corporate secretary of fancy grocers Chandler & Rudd, the director of personnel at Halle Bros. department store, and the manager of sales for Swift & Co. Students could learn industrial management from the personnel director of White Motor Co., business law from the vice president of the Federal Reserve, insurance from the general agent of New England Mutual, and law from attorneys at the firm of Thompson, Hine & Flory. They could study economics under the regional head of the Social Security Administration or advertising under the advertising director of Standard Oil.

A curator at the Cleveland Museum of Natural History taught biology, and several commercial and illustrative photographers taught photography. The chief chemist and the senior histology technician at Cleveland City Hospital conducted classes in medical technology. And in those days, when no lady went out without a hat, General Electric retained a fashion adviser, who also consulted with local television stations and lectured Cleveland College students on millinery. Painters William and Natalie Grauer taught art, as did Mary Sweeney, director of the advertising studio at Halle's.

Cleveland College prepared students for the real world. Part-time students could identify with part-time teachers, for both groups faced the same problem, that of making time for their studies while not neglecting their work. Students could respect and trust these temporary instructors, whose prominence in their occupations ensured that what they taught was relevant to the demands of the workplace.

From the point of view of the lecturers, teaching at Cleveland College was a highly rewarding challenge and a stimulating opportunity to broaden their own experience. They enjoyed positions of prestige because they had been singled out as leaders in their fields, and they also had the satisfaction of knowing that they were providing the city with an enlarged pool of qualified workers, as well as being of service to this student group that consisted largely of veterans to whom they

Mary E. Reid was a stellar professor of English at Cleveland College during World War II and in the years following.

owed so much.

Although most students were being prepared for the business world, the full-time faculty included some outstanding liberal arts professors, who launched a surprising number of students into academic careers. Among them was Mary Reid, a tiny, wrenlike ball of energy, her graying hair pulled back into a functional knot. Mary Reid was a gifted teacher of English as a second language, but she also taught literature of the Bible and English literature of the Renaissance, the Romantic Era, and the 17th century. Whenever she could get away from her duties, this fragile-looking woman went up to the Canadian wilds to shoot rapids. She believed passionately in the obligation of colleges to provide for the education of adults at hours and locations convenient to them, meaning by adults, she wrote, "the men and women who are carrying the economic, social and political responsibilities of adults in our culture." She advocated residential institutes for adult education, for faculty as well as students, to give participants several days of intense total immersion in learning that would revitalize their interest in the pleasures of study. Not only a gifted and inspiring lecturer, she filled the role of academic adviser for her students at a time when Cleveland College had no such counselors, providing direction to their studies and helping them to ensure that their course elections would fulfill the requirements for graduation. When she retired, a Russian former student wrote that her interest and concern for the personal and academic problems of her students, "many of whom were victims of World War II, without financial means but with a strong desire to learn English," enabled them to lead satisfying lives and establish successful careers in America.

Charles Rehor was a colorful figure and popular lecturer who established the journalism department and, after it was abolished, joined the English faculty as an Elizabethan specialist. He had a flair for the dramatic. When the Metropolitan Opera made its annual visit to Cleveland, no one dared to challenge his claim to the supernumerary role of the statue in *Don Giovanni*. When the university forced his retirement at the age of 68, two years before the time specified by his original contract, he sued the university—unsuccessfully—for breach of contract, amid deafening student outcry.

Another popular lecturer with a wide following both in the classroom and in the city was Joseph Remenyi, a poet and authority on Hungarian literature who had fled Europe when Hitler was rising to power. When he died, a friend exclaimed, "What an addition he will be to heaven!"

Henry Miller Busch, head of the Division of Social Sciences, had only a master's degree but a more distinguished career than many Ph.D.s can boast. No idle theorist, he had started out as assistant director of field work for Union Theological Seminary in the 1920s before he came to Cleveland. He was a popular lecturer on world affairs and a civic leader who served on many local and national commissions dealing with marriage and divorce laws and child welfare. Toward the end of World War II, he took a leave of absence to serve as executive director of the National Commission on Post-War Emigration Policy.

The most dynamic academic stimulation in post-war Cleveland College, however, came from the students themselves, the like of whom had not been seen before and has not been seen since. Most of them had grown up during the pervasive defeatism of the Great Depression, when the most they could hope for was any sort of job that would keep body and soul together. The G.I. Bill suddenly offered them a means to escape the grinding poverty their families had known and to develop specialized competence that would lead to a secure and respected future. They glimpsed a life that they had been unable even to dream about, and they would spare no effort to achieve it. They were insatiable students who worked and studied hard, and the faculty responded with fervor and dedication. It would have been a betrayal to give less than their best to these battle-tested adults who were bent on changing the world. The postwar years were heady ones at Cleveland College.

The trustees' and faculty's fierce belief in education as a panacea for most social ills made Cleveland College deeply sympathetic to these veterans seeking to move up the economic and social ladder through higher education. The administration sharply increased services designed to enhance the learning process by offering programs such as the Educational and Vocational Counseling Service, the Scholarship Clinic, the How-to-Study School, the Career Planning School, and a required course for full-time students—*How to Find a Job*. Organized groups, as well as individuals, turned to the college for educational programs: noncredit courses in parent and preschool education, courses to upgrade librarians' skills, a certification program for dental assistants and medical technologists, and programs designed to improve performance offered through such organizations as the Chartered Life Underwriters, the Chartered Property Casualty Underwriters, the American Institute of Banking, the National Credit Institute, the Real Estate Board, and the Certified Public Accountants.

Between 1945 and 1950, the college piled up a surplus of more than $1 million. In the academic year 1946-1947, more than 12,000 students were enrolled—

5,000 veterans, 3,000 of them full time. Cleveland College became the largest single operation of Western Reserve University. Not only did it enroll more students than any other division of the university, but its catalog listed the largest number of courses and the most numerous teaching staff. Full-time faculty increased from 30 to 60 and part-timers from 163 to 200. Among them were people who were not only scholarly academicians but devoted teachers with respect and admiration for their remarkable students, who often both instructed and befriended them. It was not unusual for a faculty member, concerned by a student's sudden absences, to make a house call, find an explanation, look for a solution, and bring him back to class.

The Chamber of Commerce building became woefully inadequate, but the college made do by leasing space in nearby buildings, squeezing classes into such out-of-the-way spots as tiny storage rooms under the roof of the Old Arcade and dressing rooms in the Engineers' Auditorium, which were reached by narrow backstage catwalks that bounced and swayed like primitive suspension bridges as students hurried to and from class.

In 1947 Cleveland College was reorganized into three schools: the School of Arts and Science, the School of Business, and the Division of General Studies. The last, a miscellaneous catchall for otherwise homeless programs, included credit courses in television production and a basic arts program leading to a two-year associate's degree. Also under its aegis were such unrelated offerings as the community discussion programs, Great Books and World Politics, and in-service training for business supervisors. The sole long-term survivor in the Division of General Studies was the somewhat anomalous voluntary organization of the Women's Association of Cleveland College (later the Association for Continuing Education), which sponsored short courses and lectures and consistently represented the largest number of offerings in the Division of General Studies.

CONFUSION

*'They're cutting off the live branch
of Reserve to preserve the dead core.'*

A 1949 study of Cleveland College students found that full-time students constituted one-fourth of the student body and numbered 1,680, most of whom were male. Part-time students numbered 4,530, also mostly male. Short-course enrollment was 454, mostly female, studying for the sheer pleasure of learning with the stimulation of a group. The report stated proudly: *"No other institution in the area offers this opportunity."* But by 1950 the student veterans had mostly achieved their goals. Other colleges and agencies were competing for students, among them the Cleveland Public Library, John Huntington Polytechnic Institute, and various boards of education, most of whom charged lower tuition. Enrollment dropped and deficits rose. The university pointed out that Cleveland College facilities were used at only 12 percent capacity in the daytime while those at University Circle were equally vacant in the evening.

The downgrading of Cleveland College programs began in 1952. WRU ceased publication of a Cleveland College Bulletin. The schedule booklet became smaller and put less emphasis on college philosophy. The Cleveland College faculty lost its separate and distinct identity. Even the School of Business was removed from its aegis. Enrollment steadily declined. In May 1953 Cleveland College published a fact-finding study, noting the markedly decreased enroll-

From the Trenches to Classrooms

This Cleveland Press photo from April 29, 1957, captures the groundbreaking ceremonies for the Newton D. Baker Building at Euclid Avenue and Adelbert.

ment figures, which had dropped from 2,978 in 1947 to 621 in 1952. WRU let it be known that moving Cleveland College from downtown to University Circle was contemplated. In an alarmed response, a poll of students showed an overwhelming commitment to the downtown location while the faculty's preference was for evening teaching at University Circle. Further polling of students deplored the loss of programs in the western suburbs, loss of adult education, loss of institutional identity, loss of part-time job opportunities, and the forced association with 18- to 23-year-olds.

But in 1953 Western Reserve announced plans to close the Public Square center, move Cleveland College to University Circle, and pledge $1.5 million to build the Newton D. Baker Memorial Building on campus to perpetuate the name and spirit of the founding father. The announcement was greeted by howls of protest. Cleveland College alumni and friends felt betrayed. The newspapers bristled with indignant letters to the editor. A local CEO who had found Cleveland College

24

a fertile recruiting ground charged, "They're cutting off the live branch of Reserve to preserve the dead core." The Baker family said publicly that it was a "tragic mistake" and, if consummated without more thought and disinterested study, the family name should not again be associated with Cleveland College.

Feeling was the more acute because of the tension that had always existed between the faculties at Public Square and those at University Circle. The advocates of adult education had worked with evangelical fervor, convinced that they were remaking not only the individual but society as a whole. The campus faculty was not so sure and looked down its collective nose.

Philosophically, University Circle clung tenaciously to the then-current concept of academic freedom, which meant the right to set goals without outside interference. In contrast Cleveland College actually courted a wide variety of non-academic institutions whose participation in setting goals and making decisions was absolutely essential to providing the kind of curriculum that would make Cleveland College alumni employable. Cooperation with business and industry had been a necessary function of the work/study program and was essential for the Cleveland College School of Business to develop the new disciplines required for the bachelor of business arts degree.

Notwithstanding, the university threw up a panel-and-girder building on the corner of Euclid Avenue and Adelbert Road, its auditorium and classrooms cramped and its length threaded by narrow passageways, and christened it the Newton D. Baker Building, the new home for Cleveland College. The incorporation of Cleveland College into the regular offerings of the university as well as into its campus allowed little opportunity for the college to provide the kind of learning to which it had been dedicated. Enrollment dropped, partly because of changed course offerings and physical location and partly because of competition from other institutions whose tuition was lower. Adelbert and Mather Colleges at this time liberalized their admission standards, absorbing students who otherwise might have enrolled in Cleveland College. In addition, the School of Business was separated from Cleveland College, and the B.B.A. degree, which had been offered only by Cleveland College, was opened to all WRU undergraduates.

The postwar shift to research, sponsored by both government and industry, made available large amounts of money to graduate schools and research in-

Cleveland College moved into its new home, the Newton D. Baker Building on the Case Western Reserve University campus, in 1958.

stitutions, and the norms of science gradually became guidelines for WRU. The university faculty governed the credit program. And the rapidly changing non-credit program, governed by an ever-changing series of university administrators, shifted with the wind. The years from 1953 to 1970 saw the disappearance of credit courses in home economics, studio art, journalism, radio broadcasting, salesmanship, nursery education, film production, and interior design. Real estate courses were no longer offered for credit. The west side extension centers were closed, telecourses discontinued, and work/study programs abandoned.

The coup de grace occurred in 1960 when not one but two tax-supported colleges appeared on the downtown scene to compete with Cleveland College. The question was settled. After years of heated public debate, Western Reserve University announced that Cleveland College would be moved from its center on Public Square to the newly dedicated Newton D. Baker Building on the University Circle campus. The decision was based not only on financial difficulties but on the

26

assumption that it was no longer necessary for the university to offer credit courses that were accessible to part-time working students, particularly because this need was being met to a limited extent by the two newly created institutions: Cuyahoga Community College, a two-year college with classrooms scattered throughout downtown, and Cleveland State University, which was developing a comprehensive curriculum around that of the former Fenn College, whose YMCA-financed tower it had purchased. Enrollment continued its relentless drop.

It also must be said that the Cleveland College credit students, although tolerated by University Circle, were little understood. Although they paid exactly the same tuition as Mather and Adelbert students, they were recruited mostly from a different level of society. They were often the first members of their families to attend college. They were less interested in liberal education, either as a pleasure or as a discipline, because their goals were primarily to increase their earning potential. In the eyes of the campus, Cleveland College was a trade school. The town-and-gown conflict was a definite factor in the issue of Cleveland College survival.

In its last years, Cleveland College directed most of its efforts to the Division of General Studies for adult education programs that were not part of any degree curriculum. They were usually financed by grants in support of short courses, lectures, workshops, and conferences addressed mostly to professional people.

By 1971 Cleveland College had only 200 full-time and 400 part-time students in credit programs, and the financial pressure had become overwhelming. After 20 years of agonizing, the university finally closed Cleveland College and abolished the Division of General Studies. The disgruntled students remaining in credit courses were transferred to the newly created Western Reserve College, an amalgam of Adelbert, Mather, and Cleveland Colleges, where Cleveland College adults were thrust into classes with Adelbert and Mather teenagers.

Howard Preston of The Plain Dealer wrote Cleveland College's obituary, observing that in the eyes of many it had never qualified "as a legitimate college ... because it didn't have a campus, or a football team, or any frat houses or dormitories." But it had been a "brainstorm in the process of higher education" even though it "swooped and plummeted like a wounded duck during most of its existence." Newton D. Baker's brainstorm lasted just short of half a century.

Grazella Shepherd
and the Women's Association
of Cleveland College

Newton D. Baker's college didn't survive, but his commitment to adult education did, albeit in a different form and serving a different group than he had envisioned. In 1931, one of the low points of Cleveland College's existence, Mrs. Baker had organized a group of civic and social leaders into a kind of women's auxiliary to help support the struggling orphan school. It was called the Women's League, and its aim was to promote social life for students and faculty, to establish a student loan fund, and to provide some sense of unity for this street-car college that had no campus, no alumni, and very few full-time students. This organization was later to become the Women's Association of Cleveland College and, still later, the Association for Continuing Education. The members met mostly in each others' homes and were entertained by such programs as a student dramatic production, a string quartet, and folk dancing. Annual meetings became elegant social affairs, held in the homes of such Cleveland benefactors as Mrs. Dudley Blossom, Mrs. Newton D. Baker, and Mrs. Severance Milliken, and, on one occasion, in the Big Studio of artists William and Natalie Grauer, who lectured the group on the layman's versus the artist's attitude toward art. The Women's Committee began with 40 members in 1931 and grew to 1,500 by the 1940s.

In 1940 someone's flash of genius resulted in the appointment of Mrs. Arthur

**THE
WOMEN'S COMMITTEE
OF
CLEVELAND COLLEGE**

```
Invites you to a meeting in the Faculty
Lounge of Cleveland College on Tuesday,
March the fourteenth, at eleven o'clock.
We will discuss with Dr. and Mrs. Ellis
the plans for brief talks on Cleveland
College before alumni groups.

            Mrs. J. Scott Kerr, Chairman
            Mrs. Carl Narten
            Mrs. Arthur Shepherd


Coffee will be served.


R.S.V.P.
Main 1102
```

The Women's Committee of Cleveland College was a social, philanthropic organization designed to aid the struggling young Cleveland College. This 1939 invitation was for a brainstorming session with Dr. and Mrs. Ellis over coffee.

Shepherd as director of the General Education Division of Cleveland College. The position was a sort of catchall that included oversight of the Women's Association of Cleveland College, as the Women's League had become known. Mrs. Shepherd saw in this essentially philanthropic, social, and extremely able group a creative opportunity for educational innovation. It could be a vehicle for developing previously untried methods of teaching. Her talents, like those of many gifted women

Grazella Pulliver Shepherd served as director of the Women's Association of Cleveland College from 1940 to 1960, spearheading its continuing education programs.

at that time, had been underutilized. She had taught fifth grade at Laurel School from 1925 to 1929 and joined Cleveland College in 1931 as executive secretary of the Radio Department. In that capacity she pioneered educational radio programs. It is unknown whether Baker had anything to do with her appointment to that position, but she unquestionably shared his messianic conviction that the world's salvation depended upon constructive learning throughout each individual's lifetime.

The years between the World Wars were heady times intellectually, and these two visionaries, Newton D. Baker and Grazella P. Shepherd, saw Cleveland College as a mission that would stimulate people to serious thought and make of them a responsible citizenry. Like Mr. Baker, Mrs. Shepherd was passionately dedicated to the cause of adult education and was a fitting recipient of the torch he passed (along with his cudgel, for the committee minutes contain more than a hint that the function of the Women's Association was to carry out her orders.)

30

LECTURE SERIES

Mrs. Shepherd's first suggestion was that the Women's Association sponsor a lecture series to provide an opportunity for Cleveland College to present itself to the public. The first series, in 1938, was so successful that by the next year the Lecture Committee needed access to a larger pool of academic talent than Cleveland College could supply. Hoping to involve the faculties of other colleges, feelers were extended to the alumnae clubs of Smith, Vassar, Wells, Wellesley and Connecticut colleges, already well-represented in the Women's Association membership. The alumnae were enthusiastic about an opportunity to renew relationships with their colleges and showcase their faculties, as were the colleges themselves when asked. Initially the Lecture Planning Committee was to consist of Mrs. Shepherd as chairman, the president and one appointed representative of each of the alumnae clubs, and two at-large representatives of the Women's Association.

The lectures were held every Monday in October on a general topic of current importance that was chosen by the committee, specific aspects of which were assigned to each speaker. Responsibility for providing the lecturers rotated among the participating alumnae clubs. Lectures were held downtown, followed by lunch and discussion in small groups, and attracted such large audiences that the Shaker Rapid Transit ran extra cars on October Monday mornings to accommodate the crowds. Eventually, the five initially participating colleges were joined by Bryn Mawr, Mount Holyoke and Radcliffe, then by Barnard, Randolph-Macon,

Mrs. Paul Frum, Mrs. Peter Hallaran, Mrs. John French Wilson, and Mrs. W.J. Bushea are captured here planning for the 1940 Lecture Series.

Goucher, and Wheaton, later by Flora Stone Mather, Michigan, and Chatham, and still later by Oberlin, Hiram, and Wooster. Several of these alumnae clubs are no longer active, but the majority still send delegates to the Lecture Planning Committee and provide speakers when their colleges' turns come.

The Lecture Series attracted capacity crowds for more than 30 years. The 1971 Lecture Series focused on the frustrations of women, especially educated women. The climax lecture was given by the president of Radcliffe, Mary Bunting, a member of the President's Committee on the Status of Women. The empathetic audience reacted with shouts and bursts of applause as she addressed the lack of opportunities faced by college women. She had touched a sensitive point at a time when society was poised for change. Business and the professions, as well as responsible volunteer positions, were beginning to open up for women, and attendance at the Lecture Series began to fall off.

By 1972 the committee decided to hold lectures on two, instead of four or five, Mondays in October, with two lectures to be given on each day. Increased attendance substantiated the committee's view that more people would respond to a lesser commitment of time, and this pattern was continued for seven years. In

The following newspaper articles are reproduced as images.

Varied College Alumnae Join to Promote Cleveland College

By Berta Terrell

CLEVELAND COLLEGE, the school without a sprig of ivy on its walls, boasts other distinctions far more valuable to its countless students. One of it's most vital contributions is the education it offers to adults who realize the value of continuing to learn, in addition to its huge complement of college-age scholars.

This adult education program, under the supervision of Mrs. Arthur Shepherd, who heads the general education department, is so important in the scheme of things, that it has captured the interest of a group of women who are mostly graduates of other colleges. Newly elected chairman of this "Cleveland College Women's Association," which does so much to support the college on the Square, is Mrs. William C. Treuhaft, who was honored last year with her husband by the Charles Eisenman Award for Good Citizenship.

now numbering around 1,500, is open to all women who are interested. The popularity of the group is reflected in the continuing attendance of members who like the straightforward way in which meetings are conducted and the enduring friendships formed.

Activities combine theory and practice in a way that is satisfying to women's practical minds. Two of the major projects are the Book Exchange and the Lecture Course.

The Book Exchange, headed by

Plan Monday Morning Lectures

MRS. JEROME FISHER, MRS. WILLIAM G. TREUHAFT, MRS. EDWARD L. CARPENTER AND MRS. ARTHUR SHEPHERD

found among the hosts of buyers.

Varied Aids

Money raised goes to the Wom-

building and room to house in one place all the classrooms now scattered over a series of office build-

These 1951 Plain Dealer (above) and Press (below, left) articles highlight the planning that went into the Monday morning lectures.

WOMEN'S ASSN. PLANNING GROUP for the Cleveland College Lecture Series met yesterday at the home of the association's president, Mrs. William C. Treuhaft, 19200 Shaker Blvd., Shaker Heights. With Mrs. Treuhaft (pouring tea) are, left to right, Mrs. Robert L. Fairbank, Mrs. William H. Quayle and Mrs. Hale Sturges, committee chairman. The six lectures planned by the group will be heard Mondays at Engineers Auditorium. Proceeds are shared by the college's building fund and the participating alumnae groups. American, Latin, European, Chinese and Russian novels will be discussed.

Social Scene

Planning Group of Women's Assn. Present College Lecture Series

College Women Plan 10th Anniversary Luncheon

LEFT TO RIGHT: MRS. EVERETT R. CASTLE, MRS. ARTHUR SHEPHERD, MRS. JOHN C. THAYER AND MRS. RICHARD PAYNE

This November 1951 Plain Dealer photo shows members of the Cleveland College Women's Association planning for the 10th anniversary luncheon.

1978 the Lecture Series was shortened again to become Lecture Day, when two lectures were given on a single day, and so it remains.

Although it had been made clear from the beginning that membership was open to any woman interested in fostering learning for its own sake, whether or not she had attended college, the Lecture Committee to a large extent determined the character of the membership, who tended to be residents of Shaker and Cleveland Heights and not only college graduates but graduates of Eastern women's colleges. In practice the alumnae delegates often

Billie Smith served as Lecture Day Committee chair from 2000 through 2003.

found the Lecture Planning Committee meetings so stimulating that they became active in other aspects of the Women's Association.

The Lecture Series gave the Women's Association a unique relationship with Western Reserve University, for nowhere else has a voluntary organization sustained a cooperative effort between its own sponsoring university and a number of other colleges. The series also gave the university the valuable asset of a sizable group of capable volunteers who worked for its benefit even though most of them were not alumnae and had no other connection with it.

34

DISCUSSION, DISCUSSION, DISCUSSION

'It was on a modest scale, the working of the same human characteristics
that have discovered continents, pioneered frontiers,
and built industries — the free, daring spirit of why-not-try-it.'

As far back as the 1940s, one of the initial assignments of the General Education Division of Cleveland College had been the establishment of a curriculum of short, noncredit discussion courses taught by the college faculty. The program was immediately hampered by the difficulty of finding instructors who could fit such classes into already full teaching loads, to say nothing of the difficulty of the instructors themselves in adapting to the unfamiliar discussion format.

This was a challenge Grazella Shepherd was prepared to meet. She was not only devoted to the furtherance of adult education, but she was teeming with creative ideas for implementing it and aggressive and tenacious in carrying them out. She had at her command the well-educated and somewhat restless volunteers in the Women's Association, eager for a means of reconnecting with the world of ideas with which they had lost contact upon college graduation. During the postwar years of the baby boom, young college-educated women as a group had few means of satisfying their desire for meaningful intellectual life and found themselves isolated from the academic world. Mrs. Shepherd's band of volunteers in the Women's Association of Cleveland College included many who were representative of this group of educated and articulate women who had been brought into

CONFERENCE TYPE classes in Cleveland College's adult education short courses will be lead by such people as Mrs. Milton M. Halle, clubwoman and expert on parliamentary procedure.

READING WITH YOUR FAMILY is subject of course to be taught by Mrs. Lawrence Pomeroy Jr., who practices what she preaches in above picture with daughter, Lindsay, 3. Mrs. Pomeroy wrote script for the Karamu Theater play, "Willie and His Wind Engine."

EVERY VOTING WOMAN should know about America's political traditions, believes Mrs. Donald F. Stroup who will lead a Cleveland College adult education course on that subject.

(Press Photos by Jeannette Allen)

Club Circuit

Women Aid New Adult Education Project

By JANE OLDS

A new type of adult educa- type. No college credit will be given for any of the courses. "Reading With Your Family." She's a former Laurel School Wind Engine," was produced at Karamu Theater. produced study groups to meet at places and times of their choice may

These Cleveland Press photos capture the "natural part" women played in the "experimental" adult education project. Frances Halle, at left, taught parliamentary procedure while Lucia Pomeroy, center, led discussions on reading with children. Mrs. Donald Stroup instructed a course in what every voting woman should know.

the organization through the Lecture Series Committee. She meshed the needs of Cleveland College with the abilities of her volunteers.

Accordingly she began, in 1947, experimenting with courses that were to be planned and promoted by the members themselves and conducted under the leadership of non-professional teachers in classes that met in the living rooms of members. Grazella Shepherd herself acted as discussion leader for these early study groups, setting the standards for group learning and emphasizing her mantra of *accurate reading, creative listening, and responsible speech*, as opposed to the

36

Discovery of India is subject of Living Room Learning course taught by Naz-
neen Sada (center) of Lucknow, India, to Mrs. Henry DuLaurence, Mrs.
Charles S. Higley, Louis Peirce, Dr. Charles S. Higley, Mrs. Louis Peirce and
Henry DuLaurence.

As this Plain Dealer photo shows, Living Room Learning courses covered a variety of topics, including the discovery of India.

more passive receptivity of the lecture hall.

These early experiments aroused enough interest to warrant testing on a larger scale. In the Women's Association, Mrs. Shepherd had a ready-made organization with the purpose, orientation, and caliber of membership to make it an ideal proving ground for her plan. She thought the group could be useful both for developing what she called a "bank of teachers" and for organizing classes. And so Living Room Learning, thus dubbed by the press because classes initially met in members' living rooms, came into being. "It was," wrote Mrs. Shepherd seriously, "on a modest scale, the working of the same human characteristics that have discovered continents, pioneered frontiers, and built industries — the free, daring spirit of why-not-try-it."

Under Mrs. Shepherd's direction, the Women's Association established an Education Committee, which assumed the functions of promoting and scheduling classes and evaluating teacher training and course quality. She reserved to herself the selection and training of the lay teachers, looking for people who could project a contagious enthusiasm for learning, who would be discussion facilitators rather than authoritative lecturers, and who could stimulate and guide discussion.

She persuaded the Cleveland Foundation to make a three-year study grant of $20,000, to be used to underwrite three annual weekend residential institutes for the training of leader-teachers. She interviewed more than 100 people in order to select the 25 lay teachers who attended the first residential institute at the Oberlin Inn in 1954. The impressive faculty included Samuel Hayakawa, Margaret Mead, and Henry Steele Commager. This institute took place not without some anxiety on Grazella Shepherd's part, for when Margaret Mead lectured, she kept at her elbow a glass filled not with water but with undiluted gin, which fortunately did not noticeably impair her faculties. Ms. Mead was able to speak coherently throughout the whole of her allotted time although participants found her contribu-

Looking over the textbook for their Living Room Learning course, "Design Around Us," are Constance Bitton of Strongsville (left) and Marge Wheeler of Berea with Robert Little, architect and leader-teacher for the class.

This News Sun article from 1978 trumpets the Living Room Learning program as an "intellectual turn-on." In the above photo, architect Robert Little teaches a course on "Design Around Us."

Living Room Learning working

CWRU provides a chance to think

A veteran Living Room Learning teacher whose specialty is a series of courses on southern writers, Laurie Murray prods her "students" in discussing the relationship of literary themes to everyday life.

This 1984 Sun Press article captures Laurie Murray leading a discussion of Southern writers.

In the photos above and at left, Dick Michel leads an Off-Campus Studies course on the Civil War. In the photo below, Mary Dolan leads a discussion course in American history.

tion less valuable than Mr. Hayakawa's. In the weeks following the institute, each trainee had several long conferences with Mrs. Shepherd to discuss the proposed course of study, subject matter, reading materials, and, in particular, the art of stimulating discussion through the phrasing of provocative questions.

Volunteers from the Women's Association organized six- to eight-week discussion classes, which were held in members' living rooms, and the newly trained leader-teachers went to work. Twenty-eight classes were given in that first trial year, including courses in literature, history, political science, religion, philosophy, and sociology. After the first three foundation-sponsored institutes, residential training institutes were held about every two years throughout the 1960s. As it became more difficult for teachers and volunteers to devote an entire weekend to the training, these were supplanted by one-day and evening sessions.

An essential role in the success of the Living Room Learning program was that of the volunteers who served as "responsible friends," a title coined by Mrs. Shepherd. They selected the courses and the leader-teachers to be used, arranged meeting places, recruited and enrolled the participants, distributed books, collected fees, and, of course, contributed to evaluation. Some responsible friends joined the program as a result of a fee-sharing plan through which organized groups were encouraged to sponsor classes as fund-raisers in return for a refund of half the tuition payments. Essentially the responsible friend was the liaison between the Women's Association, the university, the leader-teachers, and the class members.

Mrs. Shepherd knew that she and the volunteers were breaking new ground and followed every venture, whether new or ongoing, with critical analysis and evaluation, a pattern that became characteristic of the Women's Association of Cleveland College and its successor, the Association for Continuing Education. By 1957 the Living Room Learning program had become the primary mission of the Women's Association of Cleveland College, and it was operating successfully. From its beginning as a fund-raising auxiliary for the struggling Cleveland College, the Women's Association had established a popular Lecture Series that uniquely combined the sponsorship of Western Reserve University with that of a number of Eastern women's colleges and had initiated and was administering the Living Room Learning program.

DISCUSSION DAY

In 1962, as an adjunct to administering the discussion-driven Living Room Learning classes, the Education Com-mittee considered ways of sharpening skills in perceptive reading and discussion and, at the same time, increasing knowledge and understanding. The result was Discussion Day, an annual event that began in 1963. By reading and evaluating provocative books throughout the year, the committee arrives at the selection

Ginger Kuper, Julie Clemens, and Mary Dolan pose with a Discussion Day speaker.

of a work that provides springboards for discussion on many levels. A lecturer whose field of concentration is particularly applicable to the chosen subject matter is invited to speak. Discussion Day opens with small group discussions of the book led by selected leader-teachers, followed by lunch, the lecture, and a question period. As always, Discussion Day is followed by in-depth evaluation of the lecture, the discussions, and the leader-teachers' performance.

Grazella Shepherd retired as director of Cleveland College's General Education Division in 1960.

CRISIS AGAIN

'Cleveland College attracts a heterogeneous population
whose one common bond is the belief that education
will solve their many personal problems and make them
better and more productive citizens.'

In the late 1950s, two events shook the very existence of the Women's Association. First, Grazella Shepherd announced her intention to retire in June 1960. The news caused consternation in the Women's Association for, aside from her inventive and forceful personality, Mrs. Shepherd, in her function as director of the General Education Division, provided essential liaison with the university and had been able throughout the turbulent years of Cleveland College's life to maintain the programs of the Women's Association. A committee of association members met at length with the dean of Cleveland College, John Diekhoff, regarding the future of the Women's Association, which suddenly seemed in considerable doubt. All agreed that it would be impossible to find "another Mrs. Shepherd" but saw the necessity of engaging someone who had similar attitudes and goals, who had the ability to work with both college administrators and volunteers, and who also was skilled in the use of the discussion method. Unless a replacement could be found speedily, which Dean Diekhoff thought unlikely, the association would be set adrift just at a time when long-range planning for the Lecture Series, the Leader-Teacher Training Institute, and the fund-raising Book Sale should be taking place. Despite Dean Diekhoff's pessimistic view, it was not long before Katherine Shurtleff, a former leader-teacher, was hired by the university as program coordinator. She and Mrs. Shepherd worked together for many months before Mrs. Shepherd's resignation became effective.

The second blow was the announcement by Western Reserve University that Cleveland College would indeed be moved from its center on Public Square to the newly dedicated Newton D. Baker Building on the University Circle campus. For the Women's Association, the imminence of the move not only amplified the problems of Mrs. Shepherd's resignation but cast doubt upon the viability and location of the Lecture Series and its primary fund-raising project, the Book Sale. The new Newton D. Baker Building had little space appropriate for either.

The relocation of Cleveland College from Public Square to University Circle in 1957 coincided with a radical change in the character of Cleveland College itself, which was felt by the Women's Association almost immediately. Coincidentally with the move, Western Reserve University applied for and received from the Fund for Adult Education in New York a grant of $270,000 to be used over a period of three years for innovative program development in non-credit adult education. In the long run, acceptance of the grant resulted in the withdrawal of life support from Cleveland College, which ceased to be the degree-granting institution for part-time adult students it had been since its inception and instead became the non-credit division of the university. Credit courses and credit students were abandoned. President John Millis envisioned extending the influence of the faculty into the community in order "to build and strengthen programs which are relevant to decision-making in areas of public importance." This goal was to be achieved by hiring professional staff people to recruit and train lay leaders for discussion groups designed to improve the quality of leadership throughout the community, from politicians to PTA volunteers, from precinct captains to lawyers, bankers, and neurosurgeons. In its new role as the noncredit arm of the university, Cleveland College rushed off in all directions, planning short seminars for these and other disparate groups and phasing out the credit curriculum, sending its disgruntled adult students into classes with Adelbert and Mather adolescents. In 1970, Dean Allan Pfleger, himself a product of Cleveland College and WRU, wrote a comprehensive, perceptive history of the college, which now reposes mostly

Broker Kathryn Moore taught Stocks, Bonds, and Pocketbooks, which was one of the popular courses stricken from the Living Room Learning catalog.

unread in the university archives. He placed the college in the forefront of the adult education movement in the United States and wrote ruefully of its departure from its original mission: "Cleveland College attracts a heterogeneous population whose one common bond is the belief that education will solve their many personal problems and make them better and more productive citizens. The alumni are a conservative group who *still believe that hard work brings success.*" This group was now abandoned.

Owing to Mrs. Shepherd's consultation with a national specialist in adult education the Living Room Learning program had been discussed in academic journals. Even though the program was not yet self-supporting, it had been attracting so much interest among adult education professionals around the country that it became apparent to the administration that the university, as well as the Women's Association, had a stake in the survival of the program. Not only was Living Room Learning widely admired nationally, but, even more importantly, it remained the one stable, ongoing program with month-to-month and year-to-year continuity in Cleveland College's new repertoire. For this reason Dean Diekhoff suggested that Cleveland College, through WRU's recently received grant from the Fund for Adult Education, would be willing to assume a modest deficit for the three-year duration of the grant, with the understanding that every effort would be made to make Living Room Learning self-supporting by the end of that time.

All acknowledged that volunteers should continue to participate in the planning and direction of Women's Association programs, for it was this opportunity that attracted the caliber of participants who were essential to the operation of Living Room Learning. But in 1960, in order to integrate the function, administration, and financial structure of Living Room Learning into the redefined Cleveland College, and to wield more control over it, the university formed the Joint Policy Committee, whose primary function was to determine the parameters within which the Women's Association and Cleveland College were to work together, with a major goal being the financial independence of Living Room Learning. The committee consisted of four representatives, two each from Cleveland College and the Women's Association. Dean Diekhoff's first concern was the budget, advocating sufficient increase in both enrollment and fees to make Living Room Learning self-sustaining. His second was the reclassification of courses among the departments then assembled under the aegis of Cleveland College. He took immediate issue with a statement in one of Mrs. Shepherd's reports that "Living Room Learning uses the discussion method in most courses." Because Living Room Learning had embraced discussion as its teaching method of choice, he felt that *all* courses that did not lend themselves to discussion should be eliminated as inappropriate. This included some extremely popular, and thus profitable, courses:

- Dramatic Choral Reading
- Conversational French
- French for Travelers
- Parliamentary Procedure
- Stocks, Bonds, and Pocketbooks I, II, III
- Introduction to Spanish I, II

This recommendation precipitated an exhaustive meeting of the Education Committee at which a three-page single-spaced reply was drafted. In essence it pointed out that, from the beginning, the discussion method had been an important but not the exclusive tool for Living Room Learning, that the offending courses were extremely well-taught by experts in their fields who nevertheless were not professional teachers, and that the elimination of these courses, for which there were always waiting lists, would demoralize the volunteers, undermine the program, and cut revenues. The committee felt that the time was right for these courses, even if they offered only limited opportunities for discussion. The year was 1960, and, since a postwar Europe had been reopened to foreign travelers for only a little more than 10 years, the language courses were in particular demand. With the merciful ending of the Great Depression and World War II, increasing prosperity had created burgeoning interest in investments. Nonetheless, Dean Diekhoff prevailed, and the courses were stricken from the catalog.

Project EVE

By 1964 most of the baby boomers were old enough at least for high school, if not college, and, with fewer responsibilities at home, their mothers were becoming restless. At the same time, employers were struggling with an acute shortage of qualified employees. That year Radcliffe published *The Next Step,* a guide to employment opportunities in the Boston area for educated women with family responsibilities who contemplated going to work on a part-time basis. Such a study could have had great value for Cleveland, and the Women's Association, after recommending the expansion of Radcliffe's model directory to include volunteer and educational opportunities as well as those in employment, set up a committee to investigate the possibility of sponsoring a survey of local needs and resources. It developed a detailed questionnaire to be used by interviewers, who then spent months gathering information from businesses, voluntary agencies, and educational institutions. It soon became apparent that needs and conditions were changing at a pace that would quickly render a booklet obsolete and that a referral center where information could be continuously updated would be far more useful. The cochairmen met several times with the Greater Cleveland Associated Foundation to explore the possibility of setting up such a center for women hoping to work, study, or volunteer outside the home on a part-time basis.

The co-chairmen were delegated by the foundation to propose the establishment of such an agency to WRU President Millis, who replied that it would be a fine undertaking for the Women's Association but definitely not for WRU. Meanwhile, the initially enthusiastic Joint Policy Committee had had second thoughts about the compatibility of the project with the mission of the Women's Association under the terms of WRU's Fund for Adult Education grant and withdrew its support. The chairmen reported the project's abandonment to the Cleveland Foundation, which eventually took the committee findings to Cuyahoga Community College, where a placement office was established under the name the Women's Association had chosen for it, Project EVE, an acronym for Education, Volunteering, and Employment. The cochairmen sat on the EVE board for some years, but the needs and qualifications of the CCC clientele were very different from those envisioned by the Women's Association, and, as the baby boomers entered the workforce, the labor shortage became less acute, so that Project EVE drifted into the function of a no-fee employment agency for semiskilled workers and eventually was abandoned as social service programs encroached on its niche.

Rep. Frances Payne Bolton makes a donation to the Cleveland College Thrift Sale, a forerunner to the Book Sale.

50

Funding and the Book Sale

'Ask the people on your block for two books each!'

From its earliest years, the Women's Association had attempted to raise money to establish a student loan fund and promote social life for the faculty and students of the little street-car college that had no campus, no alumni, and very few full-time students. They had tried several means of fund-raising, including a thrift exchange and a Christmas bazaar, and in 1946, with its membership swollen to 1,500, the first Book Exchange. Books contributed by members and their friends were auctioned off by local celebrities, such as David Dietz, the highly regarded science editor of the Cleveland Press, and Sidney Andorn, a popular Press columnist. The participation of these notables made the Book Exchange a popular event, but it was small by comparison with the later Book Sales. In 1948 the Book Exchange chairman pleaded, "Ask the people on your block for two books each!"

Initially the sale was held in the Cleveland College building on Public Square, but, when WRU closed the downtown campus in the late 1950s and moved the college to the Newton D. Baker Building on the university campus, other space had to be found. For several years it was held in the cramped spaces of Hayden Hall and then the Baker lobby and corridors. Sorting was done in a basement room with a low, sloping ceiling that was referred to as "the black hole of Calcutta."

Volunteers struggled with the inadequate facilities until permission was granted to use the Adelbert Gym. It had the ample space Baker lacked and the

"HEY, CAN'T YOU READ?"

Reprinted by courtesy of The Saturday Review of Literature

The Women's Association of CLEVELAND COLLEGE

invites you to the

BOOK EXCHANGE

IN THE COLLEGE AUDITORIUM

Wednesday, Feb. 27, 1946—10 a. m. to 10 p. m.

★ ★ ★

"Cleveland Story"— Talk with slides by Elbert J. Benton, 11 a. m.

Auctions:

2:30 P. M.
AND
7:15 P. M.

Auctioneers:

MRS. ROBERT BARNEY
JOSEPH S. NEWMAN
DAVID H. DIETZ
SIDNEY ANDORN

CHOOSE FROM AMONG 8,000 VOLUMES

for your husband, your children and yourself.

The Book Exchange began modestly, with a mere 5,000 volumes, to raise funds for Cleveland College. This flier promoted the 1946 sale, which included a "Cleveland Story" slide show and talk.

added advantage of a lean-to addition, where books could be sorted and stored amongst the gym equipment. Over the years the leaky roof was repaired, the dirty tarpaulin thrown away, and the gym floors sanded and refinished. The sale and the number of volunteers grew steadily, with more than $8,000 in receipts in 1974. Construction of new campus buildings in the 1980s necessitated the razing of the lean-to, and the sorting was moved to Wade Commons at Bellflower Road and 115th Street. The available space, initially the kitchen and cafeteria, was divided into small areas inconvenient for sale preparation and full of obstacles such as vestigial pipes and plumbing fixtures. In addition there was no direct access to the loading dock for

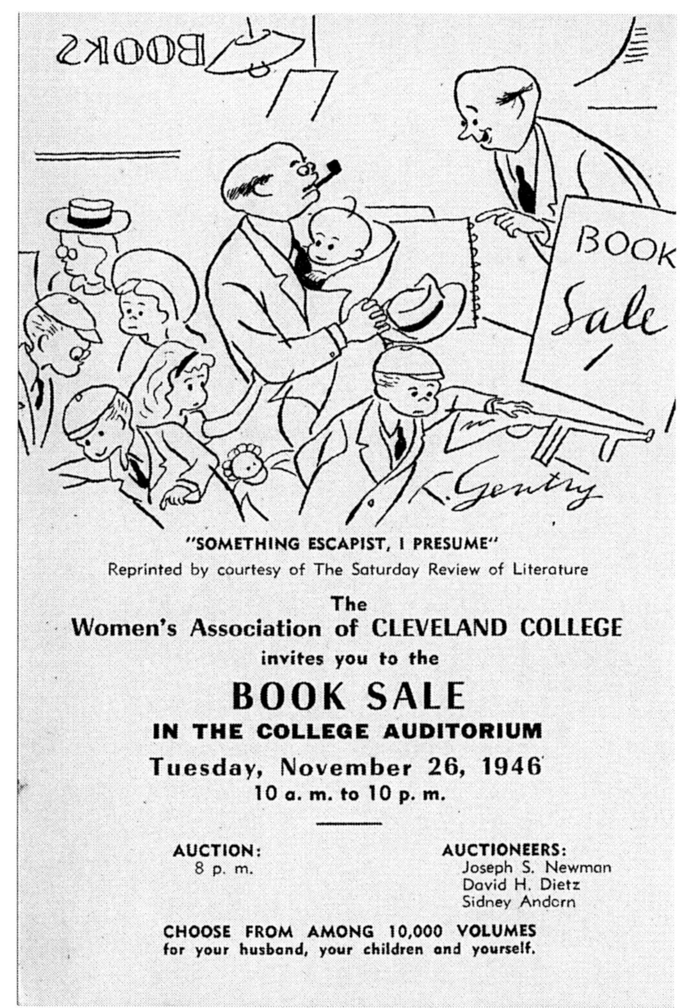

"SOMETHING ESCAPIST, I PRESUME"
Reprinted by courtesy of The Saturday Review of Literature

The
Women's Association of CLEVELAND COLLEGE
invites you to the

BOOK SALE
IN THE COLLEGE AUDITORIUM
Tuesday, November 26, 1946
10 a. m. to 10 p. m.

AUCTION:
8 p. m.

AUCTIONEERS:
Joseph S. Newman
David H. Dietz
Sidney Andorn

CHOOSE FROM AMONG 10,000 VOLUMES
for your husband, your children and yourself.

In the span of just nine months in 1946, the Women's Association of Cleveland College collected and sorted 10,000 volumes for what had become the Book Sale.

moving vans to transport the books to the gym. This necessitated the immensely tedious task of using hand trucks to move books to the vans a few cartons at a time.

But the volunteers were a stalwart lot. Not only did they sort and box the books, they collected them as well. Many workers volunteered their garages or basements as collection depots, where books could be stored until other volunteers could haul them down to the campus. From 1970 to 1986, there were also collection boxes at many branches of the Society National Bank, where people could drop off donations.

In 1996 room for book sorting and storage was found in the Cedar Road Service Building at 10620 Cedar Avenue, a warehouse with open space suited to the activity of the many volunteers who worked on the sale. In addition the building had adjacent parking for volunteers, a loading dock convenient for dropping off books, and drive-in access so that vans could be loaded inside the building.

The most tenacious chairman in the entire history of the Book Sale was Carolyn Leitch, who held that office for the strenuous years from 1970 until 1990. The silent auction inspired by her has become an annual feature of the sale and is now named

BARGAINS IN BOOKS. Mrs. Robert Hornung (left) of Cleveland Heights selects 100 books to send to a Philippine Islands college. The saleswoman is Mrs. Frederick Robbins of Euclid, chairman of the annual book sale sponsored by the Women's Association of Cleveland College that began yesterday at Western Reserve University. It continues from 10 a. m. to 9:30 p. m. today in the gymnasium.

This 1954 Plain Dealer photo captures Mrs. Frederick Robbins selling 100 books to Mrs. Robert Hornung during the sale. The books were to be sent to a college in the Philippines.

for her. The sale represents a monumental effort by hundreds of men and women who have volunteered faithfully, some for more than 30 years. There are those who do the heavy work of picking up donations, sorting the books into departmental categories, pricing, subsorting, and packing the books in each department. Some plan the setup in the gym, put up signs, and arrange the books on the tables. Some do any and everything. The need for accurate pricing has led a number of volunteers, aided by reference books and the Internet, to become expert appraisers of rare and unusual books. There are countless details that can make or break an operation of such magnitude, even before the gym doors open and the first sale is made. And there is always a search for refinements, adjustments, and adaptations

SORTING THEIR LIBRARY for contributions to the Cleveland College Women's Assn. book sale are Mr. and Mrs. Abram Garfield. More than 10,000 books will be offered in the bargain sale Thursday and Friday in Western Reserve University gymnasium.

Social Scene

Garfields Give Books to Sale

By BETTY FEEZEL WILK

Nearly 1000 books from of President James A. Garfield, turned over the books

This 1957 Press article shows Mr. and Mrs. Abram Garfield sorting through their library to make a contribution to the annual Book Sale.

to improve arrangements for the coming year.

In 1993 and 1994, the university calendar necessitated scheduling the sale in January instead of September, when it traditionally had been held in order to coincide with the beginning of the fall semester. January 1994 was the coldest January Cleveland had experienced in some years; the sale attendance and proceeds dropped precipitously. After vehement protest, the university accommodated the needs of the sale, and since then it has been held in June after the end of classes. This has cut down the number of student patrons, but the sale has continued to attract increasingly large crowds of bargain-hunters, collectors, and dealers from the greater metropolitan area and neighboring states. In 2003, despite torrential rains, sales broke all records. It is now one of the largest book sales in the Midwest and is an annual destination for collectors and dealers, not only for its enormous size but for the discrimination exercised by the sorters and their knowledge of the stock. Book Sale proceeds are used to help support Off-Campus Studies and make contributions to CWRU. This profitable fund-raiser continues to put books into the hands of new owners, a service highly valued by the literate community.

The Plain Dealer/Marvin M. Greene

Mrs. Frederick Oldenburg and Mrs. Robert Leitch admire their "mystery" set of Voltaire, donated anonymously to the Women's Association for Continuing Education.

Sometimes volunteer sorters come across intriguing finds, as is highlighted in this 1973 Plain Dealer article. That year the sale featured a 19th-century volume by literary critic Walter Pater and a "mystery" set of Voltaire.

As this 1961 Plain Dealer photo noted, "1,000 determined members" of the Women's Association of Cleveland College of the Western Reserve "unblushingly admit 'they do the talking' when it comes to preaching need for adult education …" Here, members sort through donations from community members moved by the women's "inexorable power."

Two Shaker Heights classmates from Mather '16, Mrs. Zella Fish Hayes (left) and Mrs. Alvin F. Mellman, sort books.

Sorting thousands

When the Women's Association of Cleveland College started planning its annual spring used book sale, it booked two Shaker Heights women for an important job.

Mrs. Alvin F. Mellman and Mrs. Zella Fish Hayes agreed to take on the major task of sorting the thousands of books collected for the sale.

The event will be May 31, June 1 and 2 at the Newton D. Baker Bldg., corner Euclid and Adelbert Rds.

The two women, friends since their college days in the Mather class of '16, already have volunteered many hours of service, but their job is far from done. More books are being sought for the sale to make greater proceeds, all of which will benefit the Mary H. Ellis Student Aid and Loan Funds and Living Room Learning courses sponsored

BOOK DONATIONS hardbound or paperback, will be welcomed in all categories. They can be taken t collection centers at al branches of Society Nationa Bank, Shaker Saving Association and severa suburban Cleveland Trus offices. For pick-up servic for large numbers of books o information on the locations c 17 collection centers in privat homes, call Clevelan College, 368-2094.

As the books come in, i takes an expert to decide a quick glance into whic category they should b placed. That's why Mrs Mellman and Mrs. Hayes fi the job so well.

Mrs. Hayes was a libraria for 40 years with th Cleveland Public Library Since retiring, she gives boo reviews for clubs an

This 1972 Sun Press article captures two members of the Mather Class of 1916 sorting through thousands of books for the annual sale.

Carolyn Leitch, right, and Martha Durbin sort through books donated for the 1978 sale.

PD/DIANA McNEES

A big sort of a job

Carolyn Heller of Russell Township has her work cut out as one of more than 100 volunteers working in Case Western Reserve University's Adelbert Gym to sort more than 40,000 used books to be sold starting Wednesday. Proceeds from the four-day sale will benefit CWRU's adult continuing education program.

Books, books, books! In this Plain Dealer photo, volunteer Carolyn Heller is surrounded by the more than 40,000 used books up for sale.

The 1995 Book Sale attracted buyers and browsers to Adelbert Gym.

Julie Clemens, at left, chaired the Book Sale in the 1990s. Mary Ann Wagner, Chelie Eagan, and Eric Jacobsen cochaired the Book Sale at the millennium.

CONTINUING EDUCATION

The Women's Association of Cleveland College has changed with the times. After the closing of Cleveland College, its name became an anachronism and, in 1976, was changed to the Women's Association for Continuing Education. Shortly after that men were invited to join, and the name was changed again, this time simply to the Association for Continuing Education, usually referred to by its acronym "ACE." The puzzlement of the uninitiated over the term "Living Room Learning," resulted in its renaming in 1995 as "Off-Campus Studies," and "responsible friends" became "class coordinators."

In the meantime, I-90 and I-480 had made travel between the east and west sides of Cleveland immeasurably easier, and strenuous efforts by the Education Committee to organize classes on the west and south sides resulted in considerable geographical widening of ACE membership, which now stands at more than 500.

Katherine Shurtleff retired as director in 1971 and was replaced by Pam Hume, a former leader-teacher who had been a special assistant in charge of Living Room Learning. Under her direction, Summer in the Country was begun, a program of lectures, studio art workshops, and field trips held at Squire Valleevue Farm, an offering that has taken place every June since 1979. She also initiated Senior Scholars, a semiannual two-and-a-half-month course of lectures by CWRU faculty members. In 1987 she was replaced by Kathy Manos, also a former leader-teacher, who has dealt masterfully with the increasingly complex management of

Pam Hume, left, served as ACE director from 1971 to 1987. Kathy Manos has served as ACE director since 1987.

ACE's expanded programs.

During the latter years of Cleveland College, when the university didn't know quite what to make of it, the college fumbled toward one after another new experiment under a procession of frequently changing administrators. But throughout those turbulent years, the director and executive board of the Women's Association pursued a steadfast course despite the difficult environment of constantly changing rules. They maintained an unswerving focus on the association's central mission, which was Living Room Learning, or Off-Campus Studies, and defended it from the buffets of inconstant policy, which marked the period of Cleveland College's decline. Thus, while the radical educational concepts Newton D. Baker had incorporated into his new school were not to survive in an increas-

61

In the 1950s, the board of the Women's Association of Cleveland College included (standing, left to right) Mrs. Arthur Shepherd, Mrs. Robert Bingham, Mrs. F.G. James, Mrs. Donald Marshman, Mrs. Carl Narten, and Ada Leffingwell. Seated are Mrs. G.W. Grandin, Mrs. Kenneth Akers, Mrs. David Dietz, and Mrs. W.J. Bushea. Maybe ACE should bring back the hats.

ingly disorganized environment, they found fertile ground in the voluntary organization of ACE, where all activities continue to be guided by Grazella Shepherd's principles of *accurate reading, creative listening, and responsible speech.*

The Association for Continuing Education remains true to the principles of Newton D. Baker and Grazella P. Shepherd, whose passion for learning and willingness to experiment gave birth to this ongoing program in adult education. After almost eight decades, the discussion method lives.

62

APPENDIX
WOMEN'S ASSOCIATION OF CLEVELAND COLLEGE CHAIRMEN, 1939-1953

1939-1940	Mrs. Carl Narten
1941-1942	Mrs. George W. Grandin
1944-1945	Mrs. W.H. Conrad
1945-1946	Mrs. Jerome C. Fisher
1946-1947	Mrs. Jerome C. Fisher
1947-1948	Mrs. Elmore L. Andrews
1948-1949	Mrs. Elmore L. Andrews
1949-1950	Mrs. Raymond G. Hengst
1950-1951	Mrs. Raymond G. Hengst
1951-1952	Mrs. William C. Treuhaft
1952-1953	Mrs. William C. Treuhaft

WOMEN'S ASSOCIATION OF CLEVELAND COLLEGE PRESIDENTS, 1954-1972

1954-1955	Mrs. Julius L. Glick
1955-1956	Mrs. John W. Holloway
1956-1957	Mrs. John W. Holloway
1957-1958	Mrs. Robert Fairbank
1958-1959	Mrs. Robert Fairbank
1959-1960	Mrs. John F. Cover
1960-1961	Mrs. John F. Cover
1961-1962	Mrs. Kent L. Brown
1962-1963	Mrs. Kent L. Brown
1963-1964	Mrs. Bruce W. Eaken
1964-1965	Mrs. Bruce W. Eaken
1965-1966	Mrs. Dan W. Holmes
1966-1967	Mrs. Dan W. Holmes
1967-1968	Mrs. Charles H. Jobe
1968-1969	Mrs. Charles H. Jobe
1969-1970	Mrs. Leonard P. Rome
1970-1971	Mrs. Leonard P. Rome
1971-1972	Mrs. Ralph F. Hollander

From the Trenches to Classrooms

WOMEN'S ASSOCIATION OF CONTINUING EDUCATION PRESIDENTS, 1972-1980

1972-1973	Mrs. Ralph F. Hollander
1973-1974	Mrs. Fred Oldenburg
1974-1975	Mrs. Fred Oldenburg
1975-1976	Kathy Manos (Mrs. Eli)
1976-1977	Kathy Manos (Mrs. Eli)
1977-1978	Amanda Madar (Mrs. William)
1978-1979	Amanda Madar (Mrs. William)
1979-1980	Heidi Makela (Mrs. Lee)

ASSOCIATION OF CONTINUING EDUCATION PRESIDENTS, 1980-2007

1980-1981	Heidi Makela (Mrs. Lee)
1981-1982	Charlotte Weber (Mrs. Earl J.)
1982-1983	Charlotte Weber (Mrs. Earl J.)
1983-1984	Charlotte Weber (Mrs. Earl. J.)
1984-1985	Charlotte Weber (Mrs. Earl J.)
1985-1986	Nancy Schreiner (Mrs. Terry)
1986-1987	Heidi Spencer (Mrs. Peter)
1987-1988	Carol Legris (Mrs. E.W.)
1988-1989	Carol Legris (Mrs. E.W.)
1989-1990	Phyllis Matt (Mrs. Morris)
1990-1991	Phyllis Matt (Mrs. Morris)
1991-1992	Julie Clemens
1992-1993	Julie Clemens
1993-1994	Mary Jo Groppe
1994-1995	Mary Jo Groppe
1995-1996	Mary Dolan
1996-1997	Mary Dolan
1997-1998	Lois Drazdik
1998-1999	Lois Drazdik
1999-2000	Lois Drazdik

From the Trenches to Classrooms

Carol W. Legris

Mary Dolan

Lois Drazdik

Marjorie Johnson

Sue Wrolstad

2000-2001	Lois Drazdik
2001-2002	Marjorie Johnson
2002-2003	Marjorie Johnson
2003-2004	Sue Wrolstad
2004-2005	Sue Wrolstad
2005-2006	Sue Wrolstad
2006-2007	Sue Wrolstad

<h1 style="text-align:center">From the Trenches to Classrooms</h1>

EDUCATION COMMITTEE CHAIRS

1955-1956	Mrs. Lawrence Barrus
1957-1958	Mrs. Amasa Ford
1959-1960	Mrs. Gilman Allen
1961-1962	Mrs. Rufus Day
1963-1964	Mrs. Thompson Morrison
1965	Mrs. Bruce Eaken
1966-1967	Eleanor Jobe
1968-1970	Paula Coppedge
1971-1973	Mary Louise Newberry
1974-1975	Cary Straffon
1976-1977	Amanda Madar
1978	Anne Jones
1979	Phyllis Matt
1980-1982	Nancy Schreiner
1983	Lorraine Nelson
1984	Heidi Spencer
1985	Heidi and Peter Spencer
1986	Carol Legris
1987-1988	Heidi Spencer
1989	Phyllis Matt
1990-1991	Betty Coyle
1992-1993	Phyllis Matt
1994-1995	Kathy Light
1996	Betty Rozakis
1997-1998	Marjorie Johnson
1999-2000	Elaine Fox
2001-2002	Mary Dolan
2003-2004	Joanne Blazek
2005	Chelie Eagan

From the Trenches to Classrooms

Lecture Series, 1940-2005

Year	Topic	Chairmen
1940	**Principles of Democracy** Dr. George Hunt, professor of American history	Mrs. John T. Webster
1941	**Democracy in America: Can It Live?** Dr. Hunt, Dr. C. Langdon White, Prof. Thomas J.B. Wenner, Prof. Henry M. Busch, WRU faculty	
1942	**The Peace Table**	Mrs. Jerome C. Fisher & Mrs. Siegmund Herzog
1943	**Education for the World of Tomorrow**	
1944	**Dangerous Intolerances Among Us**	
1945	**Bridging the Gaps Between Learning and Living**	Mrs. Edward A. Yost
1946	**We Mobilize for Peace**	Mrs. Raymond G. Hengst & Mrs. Arthur Shepherd
1947	**Our American Heritage**	Mrs. Raymond G. Hengst & Mrs. Arthur Shepherd
1948	**Man's Struggle for Peace**	Mrs. Edwin D. Williams & Mrs. Arthur Shepherd
1949	**Adapting to the Atom**	Mrs. Arthur Shepherd, Mrs. Robert Tabor, & Mrs. Edwin D. Williams
1950	**Education for Career, Family, and Future**	Mrs. Arthur Shepherd & Mrs. Fred Baldwin
1951	**World Understanding Through Contemporary Novels**	Mrs. Fred Baldwin, Mrs. Hale Sturges, & Mrs. Arthur Shepherd
1952	**Religions and Their Political Impact**	Mrs. Hale Sturges, Mrs. William H. Quayle & Mrs. Arthur Shepherd

1953   **Nobel Winners and Their Fields**   Mrs. James Osborne,
Mrs. William H. Lowry,
& Mrs. Arthur Shepherd

1954   **Currents Trends: Education, Drama,
Literature and Poetry, Music, Art
and Architecture**

1955   **Growth of an Ideal—
Giant Steps Toward Democracy**   Mrs. Lawrence S. Barrus,
Mrs. Gilman Allen,
Mrs. Ben Hauserman,
& Mrs. Arthur Shepherd

1956   **The American Look**   Mrs. Lawrence S. Barrus,
Mrs. Ben Hauserman,
& Mrs. Arthur Shepherd

1957   **The Liberal Arts College
and the Practical Ideal**   Mrs. John F. Wedler,
Mrs. Rufus S. Day Jr.,
& Mrs. Arthur Shepherd

1958   **Living Philosophy**   Mrs. Rufus S. Day Jr.,
Mrs. Clarence Hejl, &
Mrs. Arthur Shepherd

1959   **Contemporary Philosophy**   Mrs. Clarence Hejl,
Mrs. Ralph Gibbon, &
Mrs. Arthur Shepherd

1960   **Interpretation of Man
in Non-Western Literature**   Mrs. Ralph Gibbon,
Mrs. Sam Stubbins, &
Mrs. Arthur Shepherd

1961   **The Individual in Contemporary
Cultures**   Mrs. Sam Stubbins,
Mrs. John F. Kofron, &
Mrs. Wade Shurtleff

1962   **Today's Changing American**   Mrs. John F. Kofron,
Mrs. Henry G. Duchscherer,
& Mrs. Wade Shurtleff

1963   **Forces Reshaping America**   Mrs. Henry G. Duchscherer
& Mrs. Peter Coppedge

1964	**Traditional Values on Trial—**	Mrs. Peter Coppedge &
	Trends in Contemporary Literature	Mrs. Ralph Hollander
1965	**Revelations of Changing Values—**	Mrs. Ralph Hollander &
	Trends in Contemporary Literature	Mrs. Herbert J. Hansell
1966	**New Knowledge—The Cutting Edge**	Mrs. Leonard Rome &
		Mrs. Robert W. Hopkins
1967	**Social Change and Individual Choice**	Mrs. Robert W. Hopkins
		& Mrs. Zella Hayes
1968	**The Arts Today**	Mrs. Michael L. Miller
	(Architecture, Music, Dance, Theatre)	& Mrs. Eli Manos
1969	**The Arts Today**	Mrs. William Newberry &
	(Poetry, Modern Art, Painting, Sculpture)	Mrs. Norman A. Clemens
1970	**Contemporary Challenge: The Individual**	Mrs. John F. Kofron
	and His Environment	& Mrs. Ronald H. Bell
1971	**Cherche La Femme**	Mrs. Ronald H. Bell &
		Mrs. Richard Stoddart
1972	**China and Japan: Time to Re-Orient**	Mrs. Ronald H. Bell &
		Mrs. Richard Stoddart
1973	**Ethics in Conflict**	Mrs. Drue King Jr. &
		Mrs. Gregory Taylor
1974	**Urban Projections**	Mrs. Drue King Jr.
		& Mrs. Justin Krent
1975	**South America: What's Happening**	Mrs. Justin Krent &
	While We Haven't Been Looking?	Mrs. Edward J. Stevens III
1976	**Beyond the Bicentennial:**	Barbara Robinson
	The American Evolution	
1977	**The First Amendment: Right, Writes, Rites**	Barbara Robinson
1978	**Fashioning New Genes**	Heidi Makela
1979	**Focus Iran**	Heidi Makela
1980	**Energy Fantasies and Facts: Life Style Changes?**	Charlotte Weber
1981	**Our Friendly Neighbors? Canada and Mexico**	Charlotte Weber
1982	**The Computer Revolution**	Dorothy Overmyer

70

From the Trenches to Classrooms

COLLEGES PROVIDING LECTURERS
FOR THE LECTURE SERIES
(in order of first date of participation)

1939-1941	Cleveland College (in cooperation with the Cleveland Press)
1942	Bryn Mawr
	Connecticut
	Mount Holyoke
	Radcliffe
	Smith
	Vassar
	Wellesley
	Wells
1954	Western Reserve University
1958-1960	Barnard
	Goucher
	Randolph-Macon
	Wheaton
1964	Radcliffe Institute
1971	Case Western Reserve University
1975	Chatham
	University of Michigan
1983	CWRU Weatherhead
1993	Oberlin
1999	College of Wooster
	Hiram

From the Trenches to Classrooms
Discussion Day, 1963-2006

Year	Book & Speakers	Chairmen
1963	**The Child Buyer,** John Hersey W. Levenson, G. Putnam, J. Bruere	
1964	**Lord of the Flies,** William Golding W. Pickering, Douglas Bond, J. Lusseyran	Emily Kofron
1965	**The Plague,** Albert Camus Francis Bliss, Hugh Calkins, Rev. W.C. MacCracken	Ann Calkins
1966	**The Greek Passion,** Nikos Kazantzakis W. Richard, H.A. Rigg, Rabbi Silverman	Margaret Mitchell
1967	**Death in Midsummer,** Yukio Mishima Rufus Day Jr., E.S. Uyeki, R. Wallace	Laurie Murray
1968	**The Violent Bear It Away,** Flannery O'Connor Peter Ebbott, Fr. Frank Smith, Jane Kessler	Caroline Morgan
1969	**Gideon's Trumpet,** Anthony Lewis Judge J.M. Manos, Judge Jack Day, Lewis R. Katz	Anne Jones
1970	**Things Fall Apart** and **No Longer at Ease,** Chinua Achebe J. Maquet, C. Montier, B. Olukoya	Angela Kast
1971	**Steppenwolf,** Herman Hesse Rita Welte, Dr. N. Roulet, J. Pickering	Phyllis Daniels
1972	**Mr. Sammler's Planet,** Saul Bellow D. Galloway	Cary Straffon
1973	**Absalom, Absalom,** William Faulkner Lewis Fried	Toni Miller
1974	**The Trial** and **Letter to His Father,** Franz Kafka Peter Salm	Toby Chernin
1975	**Tango** and **Six Plays,** Slawomir Mrozek David Brodsky	Janet Narten
1976	**Long Distance,** Penelope Mortimer N. Brewin, V. Geng, A. Roulet	Amanda Madar
1977	**One Hundred Years of Solitude,** Gabriel Garcia Marques R. Pelton, J. Purcell	Heidi Makela

From the Trenches to Classrooms

1978   **Woman Warrior,** Maxine Hong Kingston   Neena Brewin
Lee Makela

1979   **The First Circle,** Aleksandr Solzhenitsyn   Joan Bussman
Dr. Thomas Watts

1980   **A Bend in the River,** V.S. Naipaul   Nancy Schreiner
G. Roelofs

1981   **Poetry Institute: William Carlos Williams**   Martha Pollock
W. Marling, John Vargo, Richard Hugo

1982   **The Deptford Trilogy,** Robertson Davies   Linda Tuthill
Lorine Getz

1983   **The Book of Laughter and Forgetting,** Milan Kundera   Toni Miller
Peter Petro

1984   **Beauty and Sadness,** Yasunari Kawabata   Carol Legris
Lee Makela

1985   **The Name of the Rose,** Umberto Eco   Edith Kaplan
Ray Nelson

1986   **The Guide,** R.K. Narayan   Anna Kelman
P.K. Saha

1987   **Labyrinths,** Jorge Luis Borges   Julie Clemens
Ori Zara Soltes

1988   **Waiting for the Barbarians,** J.M. Coetzee   Arlene Caruso
Biodun Jeyifo

1989   **Invisible Man,** Ralph Ellison   Arlene Caruso
Curtis Wilson

1990   **The Book and the Brotherhood,** Iris Murdoch   Patricia Frontini
Marjorie Kaufman

1991   **The Storyteller,** Mario Vargas Llosa   Felicia Shapiro, Hedy Page
Celia Correas de Zapata

1992   **Lost in Translation,** Eva Hoffman   Dorothy McIntyre, Pat Ashton
Eva Hoffman

1993   **Mao II,** Don DeLillo   Toby Chernin
T. LeClair

1994	**The English Patient,** Michael Ondaatje J. Mikalachki	Nan Miller, Saralee Luke
1995	**Billiards at Half-Past Nine,** Heinrich Böll R. Conrad	Mary Dolan, Lenore Koppel
1996	**Still Life,** A.S. Byatt J. Campbell	Jackie Edelman, Lenore Koppel
1997	**The Moor's Last Sigh,** Salman Rushdie A.D. Needham	Betty Rozakis, Lois Hawn
1998	**Galatea 2.2,** Richard Powers B. Michelson	Betty Rozakis, Nan Miller
1999	**Paradise,** Toni Morrison Marilyn M. McKen	Sally Brown
2000	**Stone Raft,** José Saramago Elena Garcòn-Vera	Sally Brown
2001	**The Human Stain,** Philip Roth S. Pinsker	Micki Brook, Julie Clemens
2002	**Number in the Dark,** Italo Calvino C. Markey	Sara Wotman
2003	**The Same Sea,** Amos Oz Yair Mazor	Sara Wotman
2004	**The Whereabouts of Eneas McNulty ,** Sebastian Barry Vincent Dowling	Barbara Luton
2005	**The Master,** Colm Toibin Susan M. Griffin	Barbara Luton, Diana Vargo
2006	**Broken April,** Ismail Kadare John K. Cox	Diana Vargo

Faces
of ACE

An Off-Campus Studies group celebrates Bloomsday.

Bob Burton long served as ACE's treasurer.

Mary Jo Groppe, Kathy Manos, and Phyllis Matt served as ACE board members.

ACE leader-teachers meet to exchange ideas.

76

ACE programming is held throughout the Greater Cleveland community. Here, Off-Campus Studies participants meet for discussion in Middleburg Heights.

Lorraine Nelson coordinates special programs.

Peter and Heidi Spencer enjoy an annual meeting of ACE.

INDEX